Late again!

Alan Posener

Late again!

Ernst Klett Sprachen
Stuttgart

Alan Posener

Late again!

1. Auflage 1 8 7 6 5 | 2019 18 17 16

Nachfolger von 3-12-571210-6
Alle Drucke dieser Auflage sind unverändert und können im Unterricht nebeneinander verwendet werden.
Die letzte Zahl bezeichnet das Jahr des Druckes.

Internetadresse: www.klett-sprachen.de

Autor: Alan Posener

Layoutkonzeption: Elmar Feuerbach
Illustrationen: Walter Rieck, Heilbronn
Gestaltung und Satz: Satzkasten, Stuttgart
Umschlaggestaltung: Elmar Feuerbach
Titelbild: Shutterstock images / © Elena Elisseeva
Druck und Bindung: CEWE Stiftung & Co. KGaA, Germering
Printed in Germany

ISBN 978-3-12-571212-6

9 783125 712126

Contents

Introduction

"Late Again!" is a short play in easy English. Any class which has been learning English for about one year should be able to have fun working with the play.

"Working with the play" obviously means – first and foremost – aiming for reading and listening comprehension and phonetically correct, fluent and expressive vocal production.

However, as Hamlet says, "The play's the thing". Experience shows that pupils are capable of quite exceptional achievements when they are motivated by the prospect of a real performance or by the prospect of filming their performance on video and showing the finished product to an appreciative audience.

We feel that "Late Again!" is well suited for acting: about 20 (!) different roles give almost everyone in the class something to say and do, and at the same time there are no long "monologues" to be memorized. The main characters are vividly portrayed, almost to the point of caricature. The scenes can be easily re-created in a classroom or on the school stage – with the exception of Scene three (in the gangsters' Jaguar/in a patrol car). But four chairs, some cardboard, glue and paint should be enough to overcome this difficulty. Bill, Sam and poor Mr Brown's other pupils will need some sort of "school uniform", of course – the illustrations give some hints, and we are sure the pupils will come up with ideas to solve this problem (a dark jacket and a striped tie will start them off on the right lines ...)

So now it's up to you and your pupils. To quote Hamlet again, "Be the players ready?"

Scene one
Time to get up

It is quarter to eight. Bill Summers is sleeping. The alarm clock rings, and Bill wakes up.

Bill: Oh no! Time to get up. *(He puts one foot out of the bed.)* Brrr! It's cold outside, and my bed is nice and warm. I don't want to get up. I don't want to go to school today. It's Friday – we've got German with old Mr Brown and I just can't learn those silly German verbs. I'm not going. I'm staying in bed. I'm ill. Mum always lets me stay at home when I'm ill.

He turns over. Soon he is sleeping again. Mr Summers comes in.

2 **alarm clock** [əˈlɑːm ˌklɒk] Wecker

Mr Summers: Get up, Bill, it's eight o'clock. Your breakfast is ready: cornflakes, bacon and eggs. Hurry up, young man!

Bill: Ooooh …

Mr Summers: What's the matter? Don't you feel well?

Bill: Ooooh …

Mr Summers: Don't you want your breakfast?

Bill: Ooooh …

Mr Summers: Oh dear! You must be very ill, then! You must stay in bed today. I must tell Mum. *(He goes out.)*

Bill: Lucky me! No German verbs today!

(Mrs Summers comes in.)

Mrs Summers: What's all this, Bill? Your father says you're ill.

Bill: Ooooh …

Mrs Summers: Now, Bill, you're not really ill, are you? I know you don't like German. And Mr Brown, your German teacher, tells me you are very lazy.

Bill: Ooooh … Owww …

Mrs Summers: Hmmmm. Well, I think we must call the doctor. It's a good thing Doctor Lewis lives next door. *(She goes out.)*

Bill: Oh dear! What can I tell the doctor? I know! I can pretend I can't speak. Then I can't go to school, can I?

Ten minutes later. Doctor Lewis and Mrs Summers come in.

3 **hurry up!** ['hʌrɪ 'ʌp] beeil' dich! – 3 **young** [jʌŋ] jung – 21 **lazy** ['leɪzɪ] faul – 24 **doctor** ['dɒktə] Arzt/Ärztin – 27 **to pretend** [prɪ'tend] so tun, als ob

Mrs Summers: You know Doctor Lewis, Bill. He's going to look at you.

Doctor Lewis: Well, well, well! So we're ill, are we, young man? Where does it hurt?

Bill (puts his finger to his mouth): aaarh, oaah, aaarh …

Doctor Lewis: Sorry – speak up, please!

Bill (louder): aaarh, oooh, aaarh, ugh …

Doctor Lewis: Can't you speak?

Bill: No – I mean, mmmmm, aaaarh, ooooh.

Doctor Lewis: Oh dear. Well, it's a good thing I've got my instruments with me. I can operate at once. *(He opens his black bag.)* Let me see … *(He takes out some instruments.)* Yes, this … and that … an injection, of course …

1 **he's going to look at you** er wird dich untersuchen – 4 **to hurt** [hɜːt] wehtun, schmerzen – 10 **to mean** [miːn] meinen, bedeuten – 15 **injection** [ɪnˈdʒekʃən] Spritze

Bill: Help!

Doctor Lewis: Sorry? What was that?

Mrs Summers (smiling behind her hand): Does the operation hurt very much, doctor?

Doctor Lewis: Well, yes, it is a very difficult operation, but …

Bill: Isn't that funny? I can speak again. You can put those things away now, Doctor Lewis. I feel well now, thank you.

Mrs Summers (laughs): Come downstairs, Doctor Lewis. Let's have a nice cup of tea. *(To Bill)* And you, my boy, hurry up! You're late for school.

Bill: What about my breakfast?

Mrs Summers: No time for breakfast, Bill. It's half past eight!

Doctor Lewis and Mrs Summers go out.

Bill: Oh no! How can I learn German when I'm hungry? Where's my uniform? …

1. *When must Bill summers get up?*
   (When must you get up to go to school?)
2. *Does Bill like German lessons?*
   (Which lessons do you like, which lessons don't you like?)
3. *Is Bill really ill?*
4. *Why does Mrs Summers call the doctor?*
5. *Where does Doctor Lewis have his instruments?*
6. *Does the doctor really want to operate at once?*
7. *Why must Bill go to school without his breakfast?*
8. *Do you think Mrs Summers is right to send him to school without his breakfast?*

3 **to smile** [smaɪl] lächeln

Scene two
Help! Gangsters!

Bill is walking past the big supermarket on Station Road on his way to school. Suddenly he stops.

Bill: Mmmm! Something smells good. What is it? Doughnuts! I'm so hungry. I'm going to buy one.

He goes into the supermarket. A shop-assistant is selling doughnuts at a counter.

Shop-assistant: Fresh doughnuts! Try our fresh doughnuts! Six for £1!

3 **to smell** [smel] riechen – 4 **doughnut** ['dəʊnʌt] Pfannkuchen („Berliner") – 4 **I'm going to buy one** ich werde mir einen kaufen – 7 **fresh** [freʃ] frisch

Bill: Excuse me – how much is one doughnut?

Shop-assistant: Just one? 20p.

Bill (looks for money in his pockets and finds a coin): One doughnut, please.

Shop-assistant (gives Bill a doughnut): Here you are.

Bill: Thank you. *(He sees his friend Sam.)* Hey, Sam! What are you doing here?

Sam (wants to run away, then he sees it is Bill): Oh, it's you, Bill. I'm just looking at things. I don't want to go to school today. Come and look at the toys they've got here!

Bill: But … I'm late for school …

Sam: So am I! Come on! *(Sam pulls Bill to the toy counter.)* Look at these great water pistols!

Bill (picks up a water pistol): Good morning, Mr Brown – splash! *(They both laugh.)*

Mr Sneek, the shop detective, is watching the two boys. He comes quietly from behind and puts his hand on Bill's shoulder.

Mr Sneek: Well, you two! What are you doing here? You go to the comprehensive school, don't you? Why aren't you in class? I think we should call your headmaster.

Sam and Bill: Oh no!

Mr Sneek: Oh yes! Come with me to the manager's office.

Mr Sneek takes the boys to the office of Mr White, the manager, at the back of the shop. Mr White is sitting at a table counting money.

3 **pocket** [ˈpɒkɪt] Tasche (Hosen-, Jacken- usw.) – 13 **so am I** ich auch – 19 **shoulder** [ˈʃəʊldə] Schulter – 22 **call** [kɔːl] anrufen – 23 **headmaster** [ˌhedˈmɑːstə] Schuldirektor – 25 **manager** [ˈmænɪdʒə] *hier:* Geschäftsführer, Filialleiter – 26 **office** [ˈɒfɪs] Büro – 29 **to count** [kaʊnt] zählen

Mr White: Seven hundred, seven hundred and fifty, eight hundred … ah, Sneek, what's the matter?

Mr Sneek: These boys, sir. They're from the comprehensive school. I think they are shoplifters. Look, this one has still got a water pistol in his hand!

Bill: But …

Mr White: Quiet, boy! Can't you see I'm working? Eight hundred and fifty, nine hundred, nine hundred and fifty, one thousand. Right! Now, Sneek, we must be careful. This is the wage money from the bank. Keep your eyes open!

Mr Sneek: Yes, sir. Now these boys …

3 **sir** [sɜː] höfliche Anrede einer männlichen Autoritätsperson – 5 **shoplifter** [ˈʃɒpˌlɪftə] Ladendieb – 10 **thousand** [ˈθaʊznd] tausend – 11 **wage** *(mostly plural: wages)* [weɪdʒ, ˈweɪdʒɪz] Lohn – 12 **to keep** [kiːp] halten, behalten

The door opens and two gangsters, Smith and Smythe, come running in. They have pistols in their hands.

Smythe: Hands up, everyone, and be quiet!

Mr Sneek: Help!

Smythe: Quiet, I say!

Mr White: Who are you, and what do you want?

Smith: Well, sir, my name's Smith, and this is …

Smythe: Shut up you idiot! *(To Mr White)* Hey, you! Give us the money, quick!

Mr White (pushes the money over the table): Here. That's all we've got.

Smythe (to Smith): Get the money.

Smith (puts the money into a bag; to Mr White) Thank you, sir. Nice morning, isn't it?

Smythe: Shut up!

Smith: Don't shout at me.

Smythe: O.K., O.K., just hurry up!

Smith (to Bill): What have you got in your hand? A water pistol, eh? Children shouldn't play with toys like that.

Bill: It … it isn't mine.

Mr Sneek (to Mr White): You see, sir? They are shoplifters!

Smith: Shoplifters? Bad boys! You should be at school.

Smythe: Let's go.

Mr White: Look, you two, don't be silly. You can't get away. When you go out of that door I'm going to call the police. They can be here in two minutes. Now, just put the money back on the table and let's forget all this.

1 **Smith** [smɪθ] – 2 **Smythe** [smaið] – 9 **shut up!** [ˈʃʌtˌʌp] sei ruhig! halt den Mund! – 29 **I'm going to call the police** ich werde die Polizei anrufen

Smith: He's right, you know. He's got a telephone.
Smythe (takes out a knife and cuts the telephone wire): No, he hasn't. *(To Mr White)* And we're taking these two boys with us. If you try to stop us or shout, these boys get hurt. Do you understand?
Mr White: Yes, of course. What a dirty trick!
Smith: You are clever, Mr Smythe!
Smythe: Oh, be quiet! Right, let's go! And remember: we've got the boys.

The two gangsters take Bill and Sam by the arm and walk quickly out of the supermarket. They push the two boys into the back of their Jaguar and get into the front of the car. Then they drive away quickly.

1. *Why does Bill go into the supermarket?*
2. *Who does he see there?*
3. *How does Mr Sneek know that Bill and Sam go to the comprehensive school?*

2 **knife** [naɪf] Messer – 3 **wire** [ˈwaɪə] Draht, Kabel, Schnur

4. *Are Bill and Sam shoplifters?*
5. *What is Mr White doing when Mr Sneek and the boys come into his office?*
6. *What do Smythe and Smith want?*
7. *Who is the boss: Smythe or Smith?*
8. *Why does Smythe cut Mr White's telephone wire?*
9. *Why do the gangsters take the two boys with them?*

Scene three
Cops and robbers

In the car. Smythe is driving, Smith is sitting next to him. The two boys are in the back. They have to whisper.

Sam: Hey, Bill! This is a Jaguar 5.3 Vanden Plas. It. can go a hundred and forty miles per hour. This is fun!

Bill: We must get help, Sam! These gangsters are dangerous.

Sam: Yes, you're right. But how?

Bill: I've got the number of the car: A 305 IDG. We can write it on a piece of paper …

Sam: Yes, and write "Help! Gangsters!" on it, too …

Bill: … and throw the piece of paper out of the window.

Sam: Good idea! Have you got a piece of paper and a pencil?

Smith: What are you two whispering about?

Bill: Er … urn … nothing …

Sam: We're talking about your car. It's great! It's a Rover, isn't it?

Smith: No, it's a Jaguar – a 5.3 Vanden Plas. It can go a hundred and forty miles per hour.

Sam: A hundred and forty! Wow! Does it cost a lot of money?

Smith: Silly boy! We don't pay for things, do we? Of course this isn't our car. We …

Smythe: Can't you be quiet?

Smith: I'm only telling him how we …

2 **to have to** ['hævtə] müssen – 3 **to whisper** ['wɪspə] flüstern – 5 **miles per hour** *(m.p.h.)* [ˌmaɪlzpər'aʊə] Meilen in der Stunde (1 Meile = 1,609 km) – 6 **… is fun** [fʌn] … macht Spaß – 25 **to pay** [peɪ] bezahlen

Smythe: Well, don't! Just keep quiet!

While Smith is talking to Sam, Bill tries to open his school-bag. He wants to find a piece of paper and a pencil. He must be very careful. The gangsters mustn't see him. At last the school-bag is open – and out come five hungry white mice.

Bill: Oh no! My surprise for old Mr Brown, my German teacher! Help! They're running away. Sam help me catch these mice!

Smith: Mice! Where? Eeeeh – I hate mice! Help! One of them is on me! Stop the car – I want to get out! Help, help!

Smith holds on to Smythe. Smythe can't drive with Smith's arms around him.

Smythe: Let go, you idiot, let go, I say! I can't drive if you hold on to me.

Smith: I'm afraid, Mr Smythe. They're going to bite me. Help! One of them is crawling up my trouser leg! I want to get out!

The car is driving all over the road, from one side to the other. From their patrol car, Police Constable Mike Nesbitt and Police Constable Jennifer Jones see the Jaguar.

PC Nesbitt: Look at that car over there – the Jaguar! What dangerous driving – the driver must be

2 **while** [waɪl] während – 6 **mouse, mice** [maʊs, maɪs] Maus, Mäuse – 7 **surprise** [sə'praɪz] Überraschung – 9 **to catch** [kætʃ] fangen, einfangen – 10 **to hate** [heɪt] hassen – 15 **Let go!** [let 'gəʊ] Loslassen! Lass los! – 17 **they're going to bite me** [baɪt] sie werden mich beißen – 18 **to crawl** [krɔːl] kriechen, krabbeln – 21 **patrol car** [pə'trəʊl] Streifenwagen – 21 **Police Constable** [pə'liːs 'kʌnstəbl] Polizist(in)

drunk. We must stop him before he has a bad accident.

PC Jones: You're right. But first we must call the station. Patrol Car 29 calling station. Come in please. Over.

Police station: Station here. What is it, 29? Over.

PC Jones: We're following a Jaguar on the Doncaster Road: dangerous driving. Over.

Police station: A Jaguar? Have you got the number? Over.

PC Jones: It's a blue Vanden Plas. The number is … let me see … A 305 IDG. Over.

Police station: Listen, patrol car 29 – that car is stolen. We think it may be our old friends Smith and Smythe. So stop that car – but be careful! They may have guns. Over and out.

1 **drunk** [drʌŋk] betrunken – 2 **accident** ['æksɪdənt] Unfall – 4 **station** ['steɪʃn] *hier:* Wache (Polizeiwache) – 7 **to follow** ['fɒləʊ] folgen, verfolgen – 14 **stolen** ['stəʊlən] gestohlen – 14 **it may be** es sind vielleicht – 16 **gun** [gʌn] Pistole, Schusswaffe

Meanwhile in the stolen car:

Smythe: Oh no! That police car is following us. We can't get away. We must stop. *(To Smith)* And you keep quiet. Everything is O.K. *(To the boys)* Catch those mice and put them away. And don't say a word, or … *(He shows them his pistol.)* Let me talk. I'm stopping now.

Smythe stops the car. The patrol car stops in front of the Jaguar. Police Constable Nesbitt and Police Constable Jones get out. PC Nesbitt goes to Smythe's side of the car, PC Jones to the other side.

PC Nesbitt: Excuse me, sir. May I see your driving licence, please?
Smythe: What's the matter, Officer?
PC Nesbitt: You know what the matter is: dangerous driving …
Smythe: Who? Me? But …
PC Nesbitt: And stealing a car. It's all over, Smythe and Smith. Now come quietly. We're going to the police station together. We can talk there.
Smith: Those silly boys! Those mice!

Smith gets out of the car and puts his hands up. PC Jones finds his pistol and takes it.

PC Jones: Be careful, Mike! They've got pistols!

Smythe tries to take out his pistol, but Bill sticks his water pistol in Smythe's shoulders.

1 **meanwhile** ['mi:nwaɪl] inzwischen – 12 **driving licence** ['draɪvɪŋ 'laɪsəns] Führerschein – 14 **Officer** ['ɒfɪsə] höfliche Anrede eines Polizisten

Bill: Hands up!

Surprised, Smythe puts his hands up, and PC Nesbitt can take his pistol.

PC Nesbitt: Good work, boy! Right, Smythe, are you coming now?

Smythe: Oh, no! First the mice and now the water pistol. *(He gets out of the car. To Bill)* It's a good thing I'm not your teacher. The poor man! *(Smith is laughing. To Smith)* And stop laughing, you idiot.

PC Nesbitt: Right! Now we're all going to the police station together! You two boys must answer some questions, too!

8 **poor** [pʊə] arm

1. *How does Bill want to get help?*
2. *Why does Bill open his school-bag?*
3. *What has he got in his school-bag?*
4. *Why can't Smythe drive?*
5. *What do PC Nesbitt and PC Jones think when they see the Jaguar?*
6. *What does the police station tell them?*
7. *How does Bill help the police?*
8. *Do you think Bill is clever?*

These words may help you:
clever
silly
thoughtless (gedankenlos)
brave (tapfer)
quick
to help
to save someone's life
risk (Risiko), to risk
to risk someone's life

Scene four
Late again!

Mr Ernest Brown's classroom in Bill's school. It is half past eleven, and Mr Brown is giving the boys and girls paper for a German test. It is very quiet in the classroom. Suddenly, the door opens and Bill and Sam come in.

Mr Brown: Well, well, well! Who have we got here? William Summers and Sam Butler – late again! Well, Summers, what interesting story have you got to tell us this time? *(Bill doesn't say a word.)* Go on! I'm listening.

Bill: Well, you see, it all started …

11 **started** Simple past Form von **to start** (für mehr Information zum *simple past* siehe Seite 30)

Mr Brown: Well, sir …

Bill: Yes, sir. Well, sir, you see, sir, it all started this morning. I was ill, sir …

Mr Brown: Well, that's not a very new story, Summers. *(The other children laugh.)* You tell that story every time you come late.

Bill: Yes, sir … No, sir, I mean … I was ill, and my mother called the doctor, and he was mad, sir, he wanted to operate at once. He had a knife, sir, and he wanted to give me a big injection, and … *(The boys and girls laugh again.)*

Mr Brown: William Summers! I think *you* must be mad! What a story!

Bill: No, sir, it's not a story, it's true. And then I went to school without my breakfast, sir, and I went into the supermarket in Station Road because I was hungry, and I wanted to buy a doughnut …

Mr Brown: Well? That was at nine o'clock. It's eleven thirty now.

Bill: Well, sir, I saw Sam there …

Sam: That's right, sir!

Bill: And we looked at some toys, and then the shop detective saw us …

Mr Brown: Aha! So you two are shoplifters, are you?

Bill: Yes, sir – I mean no, no no, sir! So we went with the detective to the manager's office …

Mr Brown: I see, I see. And then the manager called the police …

Bill: No, sir.

Mr Brown: No? Why not?

Bill: You see, sir, then two gangsters came in, with pistols in their hands, and …

8 **mad** [mæd] verrückt – 14 **true** [truː] wahr

Mr Brown: Really, Summers, this is too much! Mad doctors! Gangsters! Pistols! I must talk to your parents. I think you watch too much TV. Be careful, young man. Start as a shoplifter, and end up as a gangster. I want to see you two boys after school. Now sit down and take out your pens. We're writing a German test.

Bill: Oh no! What a day!

Bill and Sam go to their places and sit down. The boys and girls sitting next to them ask them questions. Mr Brown is still giving out the paper for the test.

First Schoolboy: Is it really true, Bill – gangsters?

Bill: Yes, it's true – two of them, with pistols!

First Schoolgirl: And what happened then?

Sam: They took us with them in their Jaguar.

Second Schoolboy: A Jaguar? Wow! Lucky you!

Sam: Yes, a Vanden Plas. It went a hundred and forty miles per hour.

First Schoolboy: No! Really?

Second Schoolgirl: You boys! You always talk about cars. Tell me, Bill, were you afraid?

Bill: Who, me? No! ... Well, yes ... yes I was, really.

Mr Brown: William Summers! Sam Butler! Be quiet! Now take out your pens at once!

Bill and Sam: Yes, sir!

Bill opens his school-bag to take out his pen – and, of course, out come the white mice again!

Bill: Sam! Help! The mice are out again!

4 **to end up** [ˌend ˈʌp] enden – 9 **place** [pleɪs] Platz

First Schoolboy: Eeeh! I hate mice! *(He climbs onto a table.)*

Second Schoolgirl: Don't be silly! Help Bill catch his mice!

Some of the schoolchildren are screaming and standing on their chairs or tables, others are laughing, others are trying to help Bill. Mr Brown is shouting "Quiet! Quiet!" at the top of his voice. Suddenly, the classroom door opens and the headmaster and a Police Inspector come in.

Headmaster: Well! Mr Brown! What's going on here? What are these children doing?

Everyone is quiet now. Bill has got the mice back in his school-bag.

Mr Brown: Well, sir, I … er … you see …

Sam: It's a new game, sir. Mr Brown is playing a new game with us. A German game, sir.

Headmaster: A German game? What's it called?

Mr Brown: Er … "Alle auf die Tische!" sir.

Headmaster: Ah, good, good. Games are a very good thing, very good, very good, Mr Brown. Well, tell them to come down now, Mr Brown – in German, please!

Mr Brown: Setzt euch alle hin, bitte!

The schoolchildren sit down.

Headmaster: You see, Inspector? They all understand German. Mr Brown is an excellent

5 **to scream** [skriːm] schreien, kreischen – 8 **at the top of his voice** [vɔɪs] so laut er nur kann – 27 **excellent** ['eksələnt] ausgezeichnet, vorzüglich

teacher. Mr Brown, boys and girls, this is Police Inspector Coates. Now, Mr Brown, you have two boys in your class, er …

Inspector Coates: Bill Summers and Sam Butler.

Headmaster: … Bill Summers and Sam Butler. Is that correct?

Mr Brown: Yes, sir. You mean the two shoplifters, sir. *(To Bill and Sam)* Stand up, boys. *(Bill and Sam stand up.)* I must tell the Inspector that these boys aren't really bad. They're just boys.

Inspector Coates: But Mr Brown …

Mr Brown: Please don't punish them. If they have stolen something, I can pay for it and we can forget all about it. I am going to talk to their parents … er … no more TV … no more

Inspector Coates: I don't understand you, Mr Brown. This morning, two gangsters went into the manager's office in the supermarket in Station Road …

Mr Brown: I can't believe it!

Inspector Coates: Pardon? What was that?

Mr Brown: Nothing, nothing. Go on.

Inspector Coates: The gangsters stole one thousand pounds. They also took these two boys with them.

Mr Brown: The boys? The poor men! They must be mad!

Inspector Coates: Pardon?

Mr Brown: Nothing. Please go on.

Inspector Coates: Well, these two boys are very clever …

Mr Brown: What?!

Headmaster: Mr Brown!

6 **correct** [kəˈrekt] richtig – 12 **to punish** [ˈpʌnɪʃ] bestrafen – 14 **I am going to talk** ich werde reden – 20 **to believe** [bɪˈliːv] glauben – 21 **pardon?** [ˈpɑːdn] wie bitte?

Mr Brown: Sorry, sir. Please go on, Inspector.

Inspector Coates: Yes, boys and girls, with the help of some white mice and a water pistol, these two boys helped the police to catch two very dangerous gangsters. Good work, boys! *(The children clap.)*

Headmaster: Well, Mr Brown, I think you want to go on with your games, don't you? So we're going now. But all of you boys and girls, yes, and you, too, Mr Brown, as their teacher, the whole school can be proud of … er …

Mr Brown: Sam Butler and Bill Summers, sir.

Headmaster: … Sam Butler and Bill Summers. They are a good example for everyone. Now, let me see if my German is still good: "Alle auf die Tische!" *(All the schoolchildren climb onto their tables.)*

6 **to clap** [klæp] klatschen – 10 **whole** [həʊl] ganz – 11 **proud of** ['praʊdəv] stolz auf

Fine! Well, good afternoon, Mr Brown, goodbye boys and girls, er … auf Wiedersehen!
Inspector Coates: Auf Wiedersehen!
Schoolchildren: Auf Wiedersehen!
(The headmaster and the Inspector go out.)
Mr Brown: No test today, children. Sit down, please. Now, Bill, tell us your story again.

1. *What time is it when Bill and Sam come into class?*
2. *Does the teacher believe Bill's story? What does he think?*
3. *Is Bill a good pupil?*
4. *Why does Bill open his school-bag again?*
5. *Say something about Mr Brown.*
   Do you think he is young, old, clever, not so clever, nice, not so nice …?
6. *Say something about the other pupils.*

These words may help you:
nice, understanding
friendly, a good friend
helpful
afraid
clever, intelligent
silly, thoughtless
interested

Das Simple Past: regelmäßige Formen

Das *simple past* drückt Ereignisse oder Handlungen aus, die in der Vergangenheit liegen und abgeschlossen sind. Bill und Sam benutzen es deshalb, um über ihre Erlebnisse zu berichten.
Das *simple past* von regelmäßigen Verben wird dadurch gebildet, dass man die Endung **-ed** an die Stammform des Verbs (Infinitiv ohne *to)* anhängt.

Zum Beispiel
Stammform: look
simple past: look**ed**

Bei der Aussprache muss man auf folgende Besonderheiten achten:

ca**lled** [-ld] happe**ned** [-nd]	Nach stimmhaften Konsonanten (und nach Vokalen) spricht man [d].
loo**ked** [-kt] hel**ped** [-pt]	Nach stimmlosen Konsonanten spricht man [t].
wan**ted** [-tɪd] star**ted** [-tɪd]	Nach [t] (und nach [d]) spricht man [ɪd].

Das Simple Past: unregelmäßige Formen

Wie im Deutschen gibt es auch im Englischen regelmäßige und unregelmäßige Verben.

to have	had	He had a knife.
to go	went	I went into the supermarket.
to see	saw [sɔː]	I saw Sam there.
to come	came [keɪm]	Two gangsters came in.
to take	took [tʊk]	They took us with them.
to steal	stole [stəʊl]	They stole one thousand pounds.

Es gibt zwei verschiedene Formen des *simple past* von *to be:*
was (in Verbindung mit *I, he, she, it)* und
were [wɜː] (in Verbindung mit *you, we, they).*

I was ill.
Were you afraid?
He was mad.
That was at nine o'clock.